CONNECTIONS

On the Job

by Wiley Blevins

capstone
classroom

I am a doctor. I help kids.

I am a firefighter. I stop fires.

I am a vet. I help animals.

I am a farmer. I grow food.

I am a teacher. I teach students.

I am a musician. I play music.

 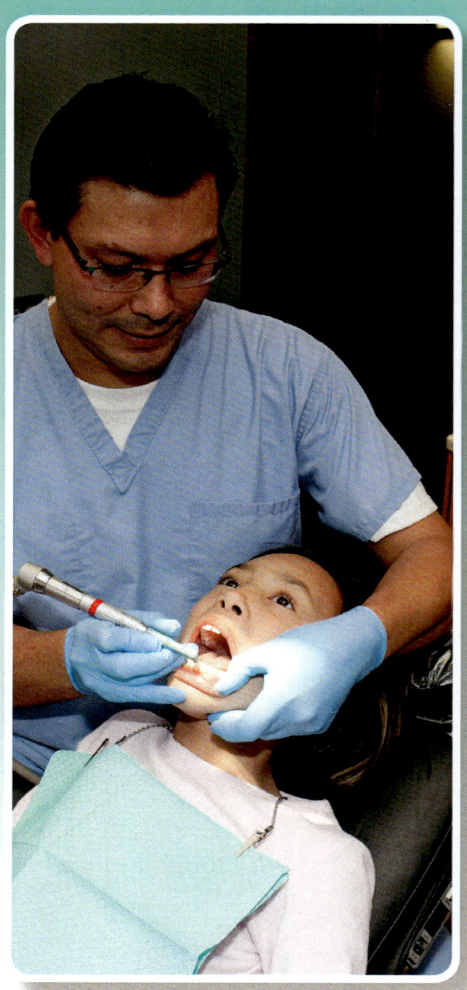

Who am I? What job do I do?